Shaken & Stirred

Tim Brown

Written by
Jake La Rue

Paper Tiger

A Dragon's World Ltd Imprint

Dragon's World Ltd
Limpsfield
SURREY RH8 0DY
Great Britain

Design and execution of all photographs by
TIM BROWN

Photographed exclusively on Mamiya RZ67
Models from Sarah Cape Model Agency
Cocktail accessories courtesy of The Cocktail Shop,
5 Avery Row London W.1
Specialised retouching by Carlton Fox Ltd

Designed by Steve Henderson.

ISBN: 0 905895 89 1
D. Legal: BI-1.322-1983
Printed in Spain
E. Belgas, S.L.
Emilio Arrieta, 2 - Bilbao-12

Contents

Introduction

"Candy is dandy," observed the American poet Ogden Nash, "but liquor is quicker." Nash was surely reflecting, in his own inimitable way, on the subtle and persuasive effects of the great American cocktail, for ever since Eve's apple fermented, alcohol, in some form or another has been employed to breach maidenly defences and inflame latent desire. As the old saying goes: "Little drops of whisky, little drops of gin, makes a lady wonder where on earth she's bin."

Alcohol, it has been claimed, is not an aphrodisiac (though some people make a special case for green chartreuse) but it swiftly side-steps inhibitions and unlocks certain doors. The psychologist Havelock Ellis recommended alcohol **in small quantities** as a beneficial aid to sexual performance—too much has the opposite effect—but that depends on how much you need to get you going.

Early cookery books—and particularly French ones—included recipes for such exotic stimulants as "Huile de Venus", a combination of eau de vie (brandy), sugar, spices, the aromatic gum benzoin, infused almond leaves and a pinch of saffron to impart a golden hue. The result you either drank or rubbed lovingly into your partner's body—perhaps both.

Some drinks are known for their rapid action, sherry for example, while others are known for their effects. Champagne, unlike most things in life, actually lives up to its faintly wicked reputation as a loosener of tongues and it was thus the natural choice to accompany the notorious **petit soupers** served in the elegant brothels of 18th century France. The Marquis de Sade (who also had a reputation to uphold) declared that one should serve burgundy with the hors d'oeuvres, bordeaux with the entrée and champagne with the roast, followed by tokay and madeira (popular passion-stirrers of the period) with the

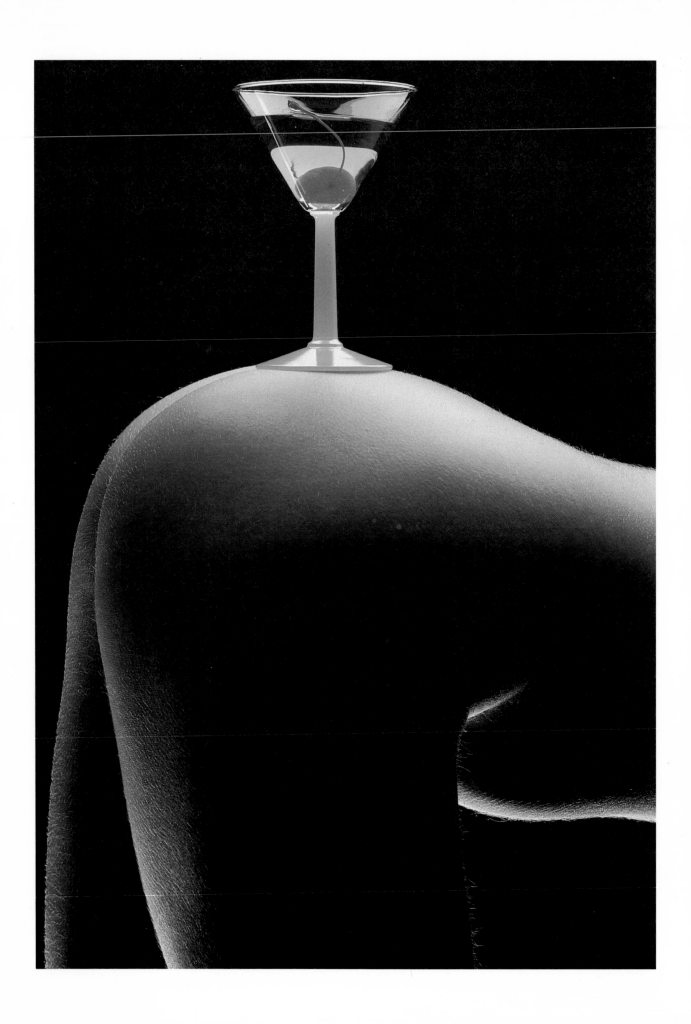

dessert, while Madame de Pompadour (who ought to know) said that "Champagne is the only wine that leaves a woman beautiful after drinking it."

In cocktails, gin is certainly the most popular and "feminine" spirit, and a typically alluring cocktail might be the **Bijou**, being three parts gin, one part green chartreuse and one part Italian vermouth—and you know what Italians are! Add a dash of orange bitters and shake with ice.

The enticing character of most liqueurs comes from spices or herbs, and spice is the base of many perfumes. The legendary hedonist Norman Douglas in his book **Venus in the Kitchen** includes several aphrodisiac drinks, such as this one featuring nutmeg, a known opiate: "two • lumps of sugar and eight drops of curaçao. Fill up the glass with port. Put it in a receptacle and boil it. Take it off the fire and serve it with a slice of lemon and nutmeg sprinkled over it." Douglas also includes an "After-Love Drink", the creamy texture of which illustrates another seductive property often exploited in a cocktail. This was made with madeira wine plus "a quarter glass of maraschino, a whole egg yolk unbroken, a measure of cream, a quarter glass of brandy" to be swallowed in one gulp! Whether or not Douglas knew it, this drink is a version of the cocktail called **Knickebein**—or maybe it should be Knickerbein …

A cocktail, then, shaken or stirred, and poured into glasses for two to share, must be strong enough to excite the senses, just sweet enough to hint at sensuality, and a pleasure to the eye and ear—the tinkle of ice, the soft plop of an olive or grape, the rhythm of the shaker, the swoosh of soda, all serve to accelerate the pleasure and quicken the pulse. The effect of a cocktail, properly made, is as well attested today as when these lines were written, more than two hundred years ago:

From thee [alcohol], my Chloe's
    radiant eye,

New sparkling beams receives;
Her cheeks imbibe a rosier dye;
Her beauteous bosom heaves.

Summon'd to love by thy alarms,
Oh with what nervous heat!
Worthy the Fair, we fill their arms,
And oft our bliss repeat.

All we can add to that noble sentiment is "Bottoms Up!"

Fundamentals

What is a cocktail? Take the classic **Martini** for example. This is the archetypal cocktail for, in the mid-nineteenth century, a "cocktail" was a combination of gin (specifically a type known as "Old Tom"), dry vermouth and orange bitters, shaken with ice—in other words, a **Martini**. The versatility of gin as a base spirit has led to its use in at least 150 different cocktails, and it has been suggested that cocktails were devised purely to mask the harsh taste of poor-quality gin. A more likely explanation, however, is that mixed drinks are simply the result of man's inventiveness and constant search for novelty. Indeed, it is variety that is the only true aphrodisiac …

What constitutes a particular cocktail varies from barman to barman, and from book to book—and there have been many books on the art of mixed drinking, from **The Old Waldorf-Astoria Bar Book** and **The Savoy Cocktail Book** to David Embury's excellent guide, **The Fine Art Of Mixing Drinks**.

Cocktails can be strong, like the **Torpedo**; seductive, like the **Pink Lady**; shattering, like the **Thunderclap**; sensual, like **Between The Sheets**; swinging, like the **Tango**; even sentimental, like the **Last Kiss**.

The variations are endless: substitute or omit an ingredient and you end up with a different drink altogether. For example, **Damn The Weather** (orange juice, Italian vermouth, gin and curaçao) also pours under the name of either **Will Rogers** or **Cloudy With Showers**, depending on which cocktail book you have to hand. If you leave out the vermouth, however, you have a **Hula-Hula**, also known as a **Hawaiian**; omit the curaçao and you have the **Abbey cocktail**. Switch French vermouth for the curaçao and your drink is now a **Chorus Girl**. If you don't have any curaçao but there's a bottle of peach brandy lurking at the back of the cupboard (you should be so lucky), mix it with your gin, vermouth and orange juice and you have a **Peter Pan**. Omit the orange juice and it's a **Snyder**. You don't have sweet vermouth, only dry? Never mind, you do have a **Tango**. So however limited the ingredients, you can still have a choice to offer your expectant guests.

In cocktail recipes the ingredients are usually measured in parts—2 parts gin to 1 part such and such—for as much as the ingredients themselves may change, it is their proportions that dictates the drink. A typical **Martini** consists (or should consist) of 6 to 7 parts gin to 1 part dry vermouth. Equal parts gin and vermouth will give you a **Gin And It**, while a ratio of 17 parts gin to 1 of vermouth results in what is sometimes known as **Death In The Afternoon** (or any other time of day, for that matter). So how much liquid is a part? The answer seems to be more a question of interpretation than fluid ounces. If you measured your 6 parts gin and 1 part vermouth using an egg-cup your guest would be prostrate—and not quite in the manner you had in mind. To avoid messing about with teaspoons, the best thing is to approximate the quantities. Use your eye. It's what professional barmen do. In fact, they measure by **time**—at the barmen's school long hours are spent pouring liquid from a bottle into a measure until they can learn how long it takes to pour, say, one-third of a gill of a specific liquor. To save you wearing out your stopwatch we would make the following suggestion. When making a cocktail, say a **Side Car**, judge how much liquor would be needed to fill the glass. A standard cocktail glass holds between 3 and 4 fluid ounces, so you would need half a glass of brandy (approx 2 fluid ounces) and top up with half and half lemon juice and Cointreau (a scant fluid ounce of each). The ultimate criterion of course, is taste.

Should a cocktail be shaken or stirred? Upon this weighty question much has been written and spilled. The **Savoy Cocktail** book has this to say on the subject: "Since the **Savoy Book** first appeared [about 1930] there has been a change in the practise of cocktail mixing. Then it was considered correct to shake most cocktails. Now it is regarded as incorrect to do this, unless there is a fruit juice or wine base. Stir a clear mixture, shake a cloudy one."

Experts (except perhaps for James Bond) prefer their **Martini** stirred, knowing that a shaken **Martini** is weaker on account of the ice packed in the shaker. Furthermore, a shaken **Martini**, containing as it does a wine-based ingredient (the vermouth) will lose its transluscence. However, shaking makes for a much colder drink, and a good cocktail must be stimulatingly cold to the point of brief and pleasurable anaesthesia. The moral seems to be: chill your glasses in the refrigerator and stir in the bar glass or shaker with plenty of ice. Barmen use a heavy beer-type glass with a silver container that fits over the rim and real ice – not those cubes like kiddies' bricks.

For bar equipment, apart from the standard cocktail glasses, you will need tall, straight-sided glasses (such as those sold as Collins, Highball or Zombie glasses) for long drinks with carbonated waters or fruit juice, Old Fashioned glasses (chunky Scotch tumblers with a thick base), and goblets on a stem . A long-handled mixing spoon for stirring is vital, as are a strainer and a sharp knife for paring fruit peel. Also useful is sugar syrup, which you make by boiling equal parts sugar and water (i.e. half a pound to half a pint) for about two minutes. Store in a bottle in the fridge.

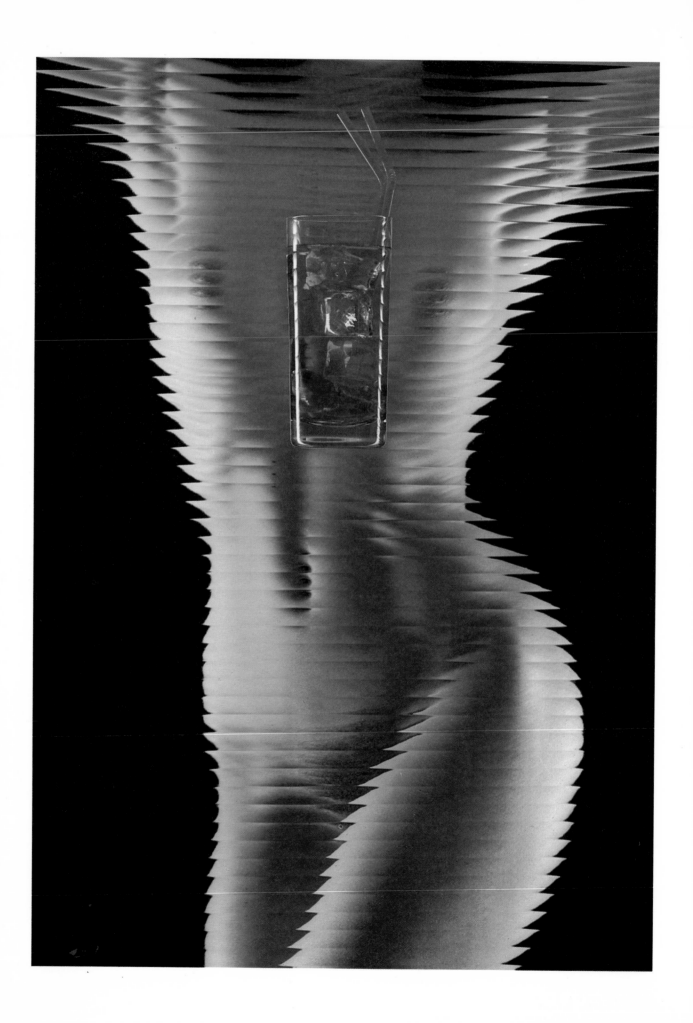

Duty Free

A nice way of picking something up before taking off.

Shirley Temple

A good way to cool down, apart from taking a cold shower, is to sip a tall glass of ginger ale, with a dash of grenadine, over ice cubes.

    Shirley Jane, however, is Shirley Temple's naughty sister. She holds onto the grenadine but replaces the ginger ale with as much rye whisky as she dares—plus a spoonful of sugar to make the medicine go down.

Mack The Knife

Commonly known as the **Bartender**, this is the sort of cocktail that goes for the throat or at best stretches you out on the floor. We have included it to show the desperate measures to which some barmen are driven in order to find a new way of dislocating the nervous system. The cocktail (it's a cocktail?) comprises equal parts of gin, dry sherry, French vermouth and Dubonnet, with a dash of curaçao or Grand Marnier for seasoning. It is a variation on the classic **Baron**, but with the addition of sherry, and Dubonnet in place of sweet vermouth.

13

Golden Screw

This was invented in the days when a screw was something that held two planks together, being an **Orange Blossom** made with vodka instead of gin:

> 1 part vodka
> 3 parts orange juice

The modern version, however, goes as follows:

> 1 part Drambuie
> 1 part Lemon Hart rum
> 1 part dry sherry

Stir with ice in a bar glass, strain into cocktail glasses, and drop a delicate spiral of lemon peel into each. The blonde is optional.

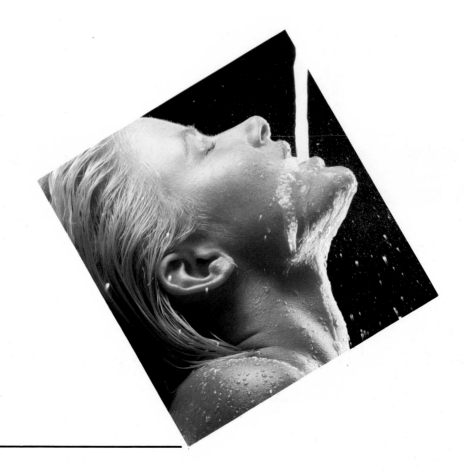

Shorts

The advantage of shorts, or briefs if you prefer, is that they are easy to take—or rather put—down. A short drink is simply a quick one: scotch on the rocks, pink gin, **Martini** or any other mixture which bypasses such frills as fruit juice, egg white, coconut cream or anything else that would get in the way of the alcohol. **Highballs** are liquor based drinks topped up with a carbonated beverage, like a gin and tonic or a whisky and ginger ale, but they are not short, or even low. **Slings** and **daisies** are not short, nor are **fixes** and **rickeys**, **bucks** and **collinses**. Delicious though they may be, all these go for the slow burn ... Let's hear it for the short, sharp shock!

Banana Bliss

A simple brandy cocktail, related to the
Stinger (see page 55), Banana Bliss
comprises equal parts of crème de banane
and brandy. If this is too sweet for your taste,
increase the brandy and add a dash of
Angostura bitters. Shake with ice and strain
into a cocktail glass. Drink slowly, while
peeling off.

Chocolate Soldier

2 parts Dubonnet
4 parts gin
1 part lime juice

Moist, brown and clinging, this cocktail is improved if served in the bed in preference to on the rocks. Pour the ingredients into a shaker with ice. Turn down the lights, turn up the music, and shake to a fast beat.

Scotch On The Rocks

Scotsmen usually prefer to pursue their pleasures in comfort as having it on the rocks is wet and windy. This is known in America as coming through the rye.

Dizzy Dame

Not so much from the high life as the effect on the more responsive areas of the body of this concoction:

    1 part brandy
    1 part kahlua or Tia Maria
    dash cherry brandy
    1 part cream

Shake together with ice, pour into a goblet and, as a precaution, administer while horizontal.

Whisky Mac

This is perhaps the only true Hibernian cocktail. Admittedly the **Bobby Burns** (equal parts whisky and Drambuie), has its adherents as does this recently unearthed 19th century recipe:

½ gill whisky
1 teaspoon bitters
2 drops essence of cinnamon
sugar syrup to sweeten
½lb ice, pounded

The Whisky Mac itself is a cold-weather drink for when there's a nip in the air and you prefer staying in bed. It is made as follows:

2 parts Scotch whisky
1 part ginger wine

Some people add a dash of hot water.

Dry Martini

For many, the ultimate cocktail, and companion to the **Manhattan**. Historians of the cocktail tell us that the Martini was originally called the **Martinez** and was made with sweet, Italian vermouth instead of the usual dry, French vermouth. There are no strict rules for making a Martini cocktail, since tastes vary, but the general guidelines are as follows: use the best quality gin and a good French vermouth such as Noilly Prat (dry sherry is an excellent substitute) in the ratio of 1 part vermouth to 6 or 7 parts gin. Equal parts of gin and vermouth is not recognised as a Martini but simply as a **Gin And French**. Some cocktail fanciers keep their gin in the refrigerator, and add the vermouth with an eye dropper, or merely pass the vermouth cork over the glass. We do not advocate such mean measures. If you want a Martini **that** dry, use an umbrella ...

The cocktail should be refreshingly frosty but never frigid, and stirred, not shaken. Why? Because shaking dilutes the alcohol more than if you stir it with ice in a suitable container, and shaking may rob the Martini of its characteristic, crystalline translucence and create a cloudy appearance. (David Embury, ultimate authority on the Martini, says that if you shake a Martini instead of stirring it, the drink is known as a **Bradford**.) A twist of lemon peel over the surface, and the addition of a green olive completes the picture—a masterpiece. In New York city, where the Martini is held in the highest esteem, drinkers sometimes refuse the olive, commanding the barman to "hold the fruit", since they maintain the olive displaces the liquor, lowers the temperature, and soaks up some of the precious liquid. The more brusque, hard-edged customers may be heard to snarl, "When I want a fruit salad I'll ask for it."

A cocktail pearl onion in place of the olive produces a **Gibson** cocktail.

The Rose

1 part dry vermouth
1 part grenadine, cherry brandy or something equally pink
4 parts gin

Pour into a mixing glass, add ice and stir in a provocative fashion. The Rose turns pink those parts which other cocktails cannot reach ...

Bloody Mary

Before, during or the morning after, this versatile mixture would soften even the stony heart of the Queen whose name it bears:

> 1 part vodka
> 4 parts tomato juice
> couple of dashes Worcestershire sauce
> dash lemon juice
> pinch celery salt
> salt and pepper to taste

Substitute beef bouillon or condensed consommé for the tomato juice and you have a **Bullshot**, half and half and it's a **Bloodshot** (which is probably how you'll feel when you wish you hadn't).

Golden Slipper

The classic recipe for this drink calls for a measure of yellow chartreuse to be poured into a **pousse café** glass (or any tall, straight-sided glass on a stem) followed by an egg yolk (broken) floated on top and finally a measure of Danzig Goldwasser, poured over the back of a teaspoon. It was a drink specially created for the **poule de luxe,** the girl who has everything—and more where that came from.

Pousse cafés (literally: to push coffee down) are made up of liqueurs selected for their colour and different densities, poured by turn (heaviest first) so that they remain in layers, an operation for which you need patience and a steady hand. For a drink destined for the bedroom, however, when you can't rely on a steady anything, try this variation: equal parts yellow chartreuse and either apricot or peach brandy, thoroughly shaken with ice. The result will be divinely sweet, as smooth as a silk stocking and guaranteed to make her toes curl.

Midnight

This is the drink to have ready when both hands are pointing upwards; it will keep them occupied for a breathing space:

2 demi-tasse cups of black coffee
1 measure Tia Maria
Whipped cream

Pour the liqueur into the coffee and float the whipped cream on top. (Is this a Cuban or Jamaican coffee?)

Mixing

The one-handed horizontal shake, as well as giving the practitioner a new angle on things, will ensure that they mix in the most interesting circles (not to mention up and down!)

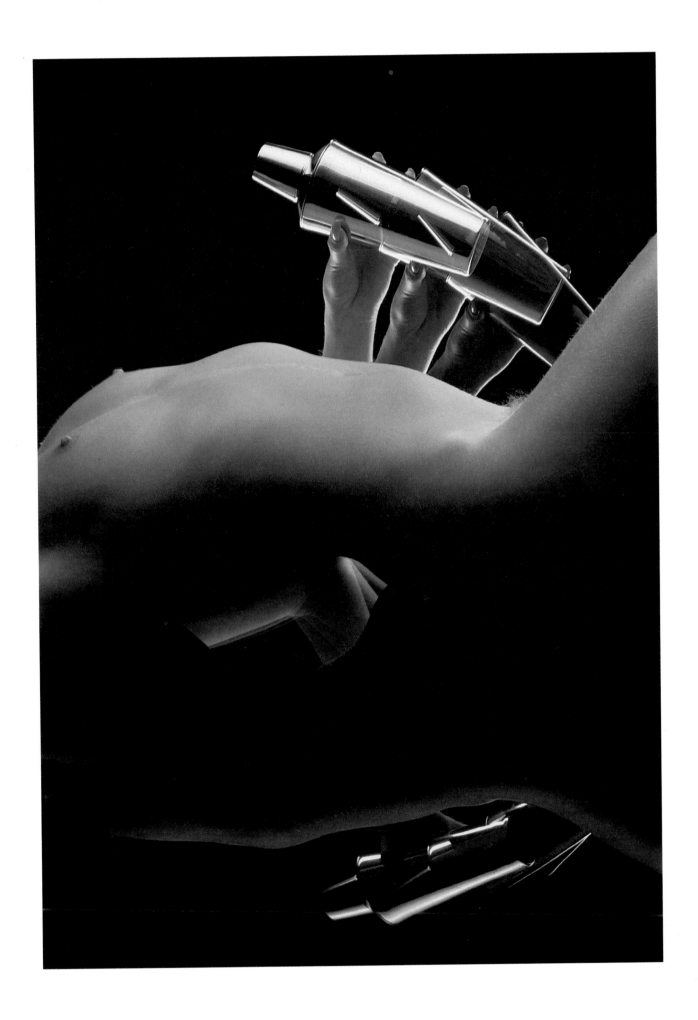

Night Light

For those who prefer not to feel their way in the dark we recommend the following:

  2 parts white rum
  1 part orange curaçao
  1 egg yolk for each two drinks

Shake ingredients well with ice, and strain into goblets.

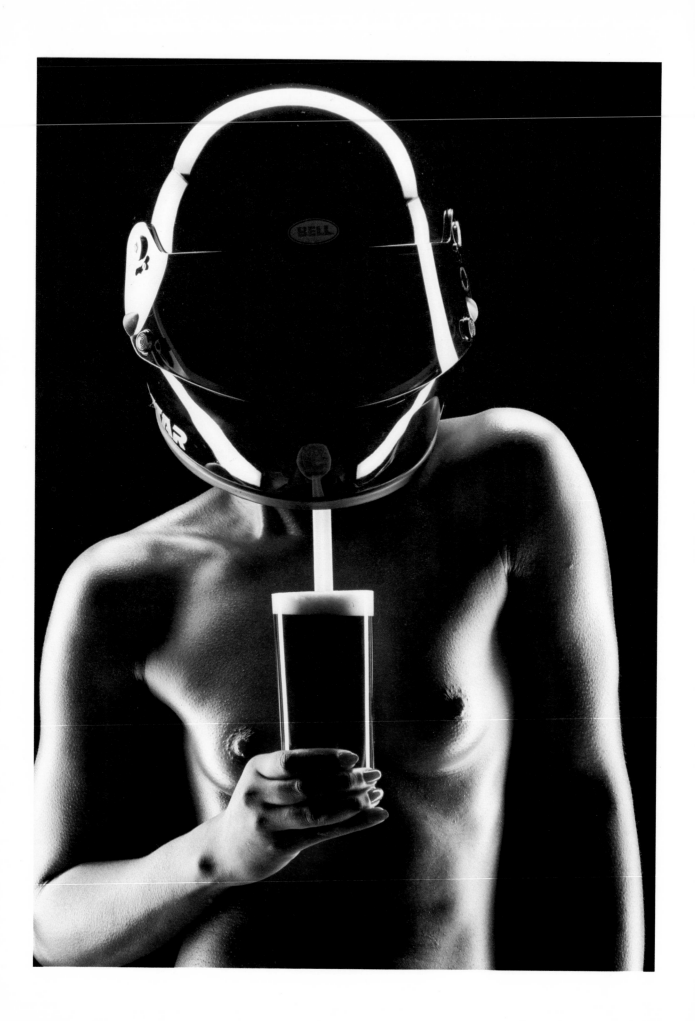

Black Velvet

Pour equal parts of champagne and Guinness stout simultaneously into a tall glass with a steady hand. Called variously **Champagne Velvet**, **Velvet**, or sometimes **Bismarck**, the combination results in a very black, very smooth and satiny drink with a concealed effervescence that imparts a tingling sensation to the tongue, and elsewhere. It is also an ideal drink for the "morning after".

Mix-Up

Being the polite name for any cocktail that
involves an inordinate number of
ingredients. A fine example is the
Almagoozlum which might, in wine circles,
be considered as made from bin ends:

> 1 part Holland Gin
> 4 parts water
> 3 parts sugar syrup
> 3 parts yellow chartreuse
> 3 parts Jamaica rum
> 1 egg white for each two drinks
> 1 part curaçao
> 1 part bitters

Shake with crushed ice, strain into chilled
glasses, light the blue touch-paper and
stand well back!

Silk Stockings

Basically an **Alexander**, with tequila instead of the gin, this cocktail is more in the nature of a dessert than a drink and may be best tackled with a spoon:

> 4 parts tequila
> 2 parts white crème de menthe
> dash of grenadine
> generous measure cream

Put all ingredients into a blender with lots of ice. Turn it on full speed ahead and when nicely mixed and frothy, pour into glasses. Sprinkle with a little cinnamon and garnish with a garter.

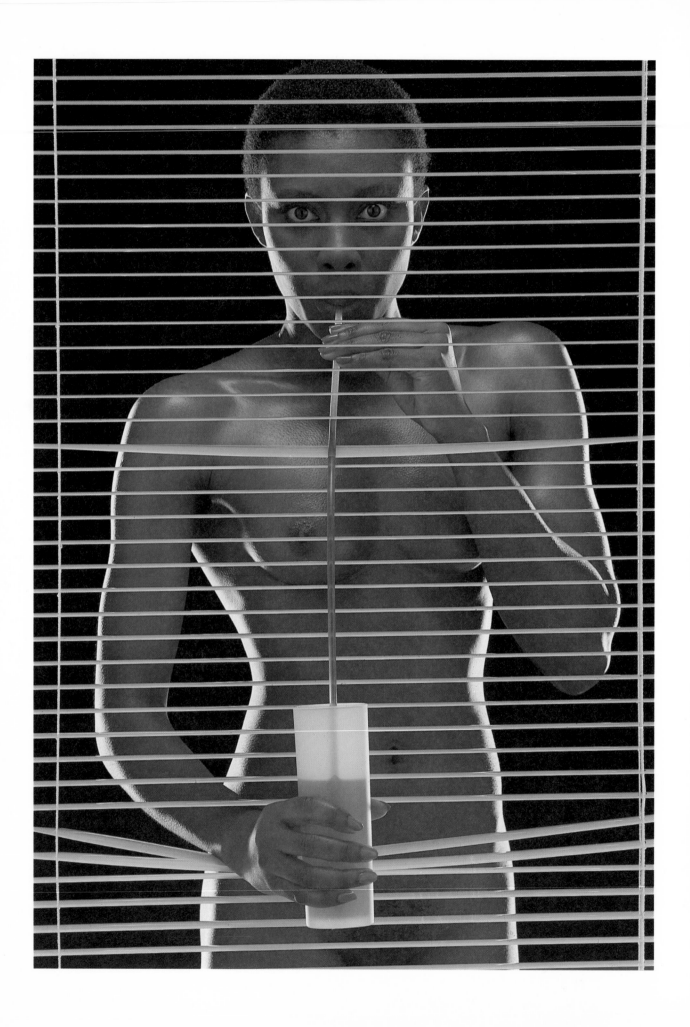

Venetian Sling

2 parts gin
1 part Campari
1 part Galliano

Stir, pour over ice and top up with soda.
Also known in some circles as **Blind Man's
Buff**, this variation on the classic **Singapore
Sling** might not get you as far as the
mysterious East, but you'll be floating down
the Grand Canal in no time.

Fun In Bed

1 part brandy
1 part grape juice

Shaken with ice, this might not be quite what the Little Fellow had in mind but Good-Time Charlie would certainly approve.

Pink Pussy

2 parts Campari
1 part peach brandy
1 egg white to every two drinks

Put all the ingredients into a shaker with ice.
Agitate until well blended, thick and creamy,
and eject into chilled glasses.

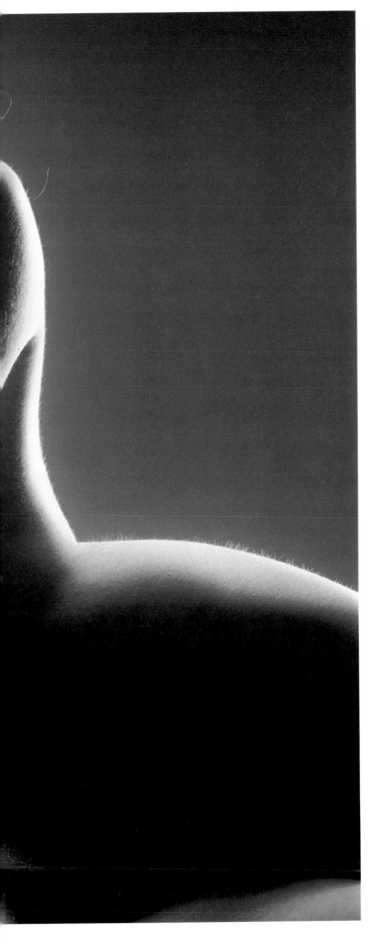

Brandy

Brandy, and someone to share it with, is better suited to Intermission than Overture. Those who like their brandy au naturel might be interested to know that after many years of exhaustive (and exhausting) research, experts have finally concluded that the perfect receptacle for this most aromatic of spirits is the human navel. Unbreakable, unspillable (if kept firmly in the horizontal position) and with a built-in warming device, it might not hold as much as the conventional brandy glass, but it makes drinking much more fun.

More energetic readers might care to try their brandy chilled; as a **Stinger**, for example:

2 parts brandy
1 part white crème de menthe

Stir with cracked ice and serve either straight or on the rocks.

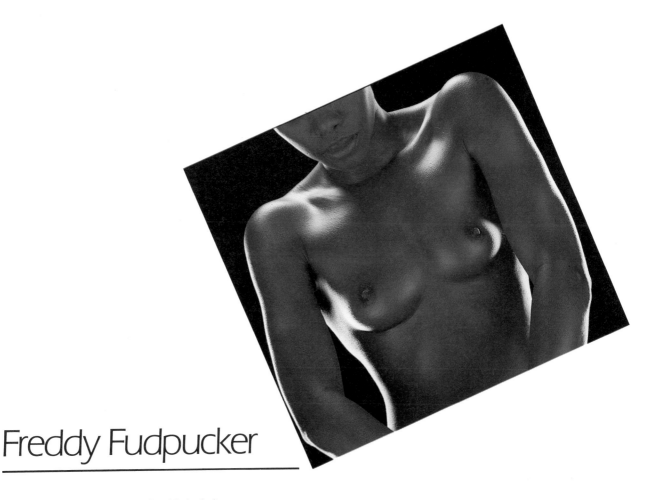

Freddy Fudpucker

Tequilla, the basis of this drink, is by no means everybody's cup of tea, and the practise of drinking it with salt and a squeeze of lemon juice is simply to disguise the flavour of the crude spirit.

Another way to do this is to dilute it with orange juice and sweeten with a liqueur, such as the newly-arrived Galliano, used in the **Harvey Wallbanger**. Harvey's lesser known cousin, Freddy Fudpucker, is constructed from the following:

    1 part tequilla
    orange juice
    1 part Galliano

Shake well with ice, and serve with a straw or two.

Fudpucker is, of course, the anagram of Duckprufe.

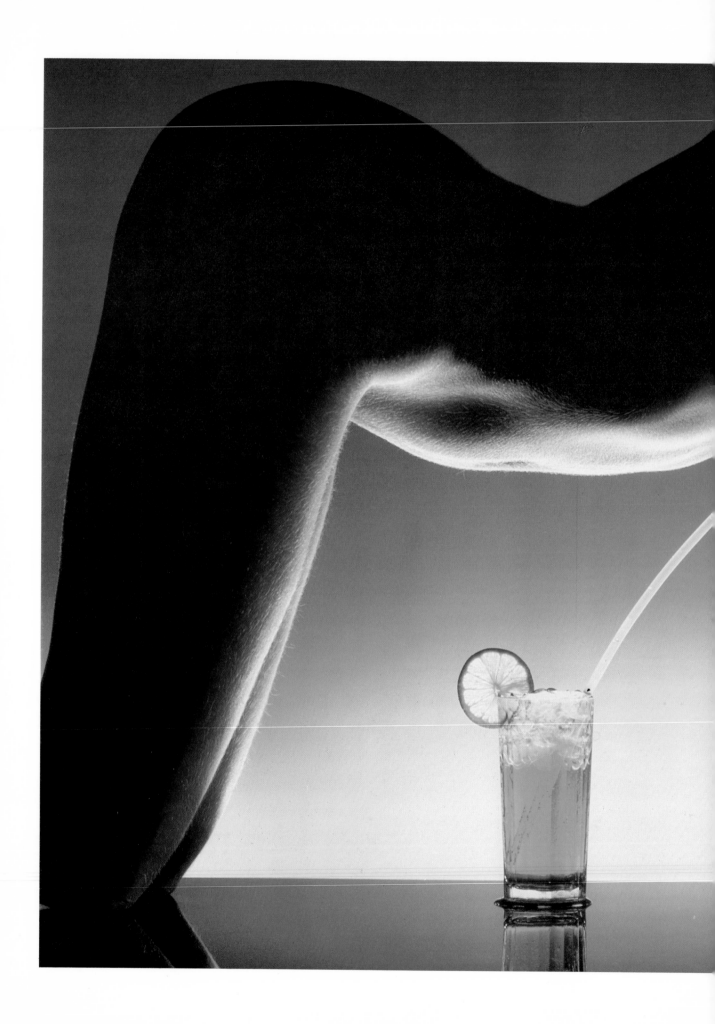

Blue Lagoon

1 part blue curaçao
1 part vodka
lemonade

This may have been named after the popular novel (later the subject of two movies) by De Vere Stacpoole about a boy and girl shipwrecked on a desert island who grow to adulthood without the benefit of sex education.

Curaçao is an orange-based liqueur from the Dutch West Indies, so the Blue Lagoon theme is appropriate, but for a more tropical effect we suggest you try replacing the vodka with white rum, such as Bacardi. Serve it on the rocks, with plenty of ice.

If you omit the lemonade and present the drink in a cocktail glass, you have a **Blue Monday**.

Bamboo

This is a wine-based and non-spiritous (though not entirely spiritless—both vermouth and sherry are fortified wines) cocktail, also known as **Amour**, which, as every schoolboy knows, is French. The **Old Waldorf-Astoria Bar Book** lists this cocktail as the **Armour**. So, if either amour, or even armour (though chain mail is more flexible) is what you need, then stir together the following:

1 part dry sherry
1 part French vermouth
dash of orange bitters

Pour over ice cubes and serve with a twist of lemon. Replace the dry vermouth with sweet and you have an **Adonis**.

What is done with the bamboo is, of course, up to you ...

Pink Lady

1 part grenadine
2 parts lemon juice
2 parts applejack brandy
5 parts gin
1 egg white to each two drinks

Shake all together with ice, strain into cocktail glasses, and if she doesn't turn pink, she's no lady.

Black Mischief

1 part grape juice
1 part Mandarine Napoléon
(tangerine liqueur)

Mix and top up with chilled, sparkling white wine. Drop one black grape into the glass, split another and balance it on the rim.

Between The Sheets

1 part Cointreau
2 parts lime juice
3 parts brandy
3 parts rum

Shake all together with crushed ice. Add a
twist of lemon peel if desired. Enough said.

Blue Lady

Based on the famous **White Lady**, invented in Paris at the start of the 1920s, itself a variation on the basic **Gin Sour**, the thoroughly modern Blue Lady uses blue curaçao instead of Cointreau as follows:

1 part fresh lemon juice
2 parts blue curaçao
7 to 8 parts gin
1 egg white to each two drinks

Shake all ingredients passionately with ice until creamy and cold, but not frigid. A blue lady could do with warming up, but if the above should fail to ignite her, there are other ways...

Damn The Weather

(A drink to rekindle interest in old flames.)

  1 part orange juice
  1 part Italian vermouth
  5 parts gin
  3 dashes orange curaçao

Shake the above vigorously with ice, strain into a goblet and decorate with slices of orange and a cherry. The orange juice refreshes, the dry vermouth balances the sweetness of the fruit and the curaçao, and the gin holds it all together.

The fireside, by the way, has long been associated with feminine warmth and fecundity, especially in ancient Rome, where the goddess Fornax ruled the hearth. A **fornax** was a hearth or oven—a **fornix** was a brothel.

Refreshers

Tall, long, cool drinks, usually with a carbonated beverage, refresh, revive and rejuvenate, so that you can, in effect, take up again more or less where you left off.

A **Highball** is any spirit diluted with a fizzy partner, such as Scotch and soda or gin and tonic, or the famous **Horse's Neck**: your choice of spirit in a tall glass, filled up with ginger ale, ice and a spiral of lemon peel draped over the edge of the glass—on the inside, of course.

A **Buck** is gin, ginger ale and lemon juice with ice.

A **Rickey** is a choice of spirit with fresh lime juice, plus sugar syrup and a sweet liqueur.

A **Collins** is a tall drink of spirit—such as gin—with lemon juice, sugar syrup, soda water and ice.

A **Fizz** is made with the same ingredients as a **Collins**, but should be very well iced, and charged with very fizzy, foaming soda water.

Corpse Reviver

Supposedly a means of bringing the dead (drunk?) back to life or, alternatively, delivering the **coup de grace**, the following may have been what Dr Frankenstein used:

   1 part arrack or Swedish Punch (a blend of rum and aquavit)
   1 part Cointreau
   3 parts gin
   1 part Pernod
   1 part lemon juice

Shake until you peacefully expire.
   A gentler reviver is this recipe:

   1 part brandy
   4 parts milk
   dash of Angostura bitters
   sugar to sweeten

Pour into a goblet, stir and top up with soda water. Once there is a sign of life, help her back to bed.

Up In Mabel's Room

1 part grapefruit juice
1 part golden, runny honey
2 parts bourbon whisky

Mabel was the extremely accommodating barmaid at New York's Hartford hotel during the 1940s. Her instructions were to "shake with cracked ice, strain into a cocktail glass, decorate with a cherry and a grapefruit segment, and take it lying down."

Fallen Angel

This variation on the **Gin Sour**, minus the bitters, is also known as a **Greenback**:

7 parts gin
2 parts green crème de menthe
juice of a lemon or lime
dash of Angostura bitters

Shake well with ice and strain into cocktail glasses, and add to each a green maraschino cherry. This drink's distinctly greenish tinge is in deference to the envy of all those who wish they'd fallen too.

Index